A Guide to
Communication
&
Influencing

Table of Contents

Introduction

Hello, my name is Gavin. You may know me if you've attended one of my courses, been coached by me or listened to my podcasts on iTunes. For those of you who haven't; nice to meet you.

This is the 4th in the 'A Guide to...' series looking at Communication & Influencing.

The plan is to produce a full set of personal, management & leadership development guides. They should all take less than an hour to read, be very practical and cover all the essentials I've picked up while working with over 10,000 people (through a mix of training/coaching and leading). I have a background in Managing & Leading large numbers of people; the content of each book is grounded in practical reality.

Books produced so far:

Book 1: A Guide to Motivation, Happiness, Success & Resilience
Book 2: A Guide to Team Development
Book 3: A Guide to Difficult Conversations
Book 4: A Guide to Communication & Influencing

To come:
A Guide to Managing Time
A Guide to Coaching & Delegation
A Guide to Leadership
A Guide to Personality Type

.... and maybe a few more.

This book is divided into two parts:

- Part 1 Communication

- Part 2 Influencing

Part 1 Communication

How important is communication in your job or your home life?

I've asked this question to thousands of people I've worked with around the world; the resounding answer is always 'it's probably the most important part of my job, even my life'.

The next obvious question would be 'how much time have you spent studying the art of communication, bearing in mind it's the most important part of your life'?

You may be thinking 'alright smart arse, give me a break, yes I don't know everything about communication, at least I'm reading this book'. Or you may be thinking 'gosh, he's got a point, what kind of idiot am I for overlooking such an important matter for so long'. Or you may be contemplating what to have for dinner tonight. Or thinking you've been backed into a corner or set a trap with the first question and defenceless in your reply to the second (Day 2 of a sales course from the 1980s).

When I'm training people on communication & influencing I like to ask how important communication is to them quite early on in the session, but not till I've got them on my side, not until I understand them, not until I've built rapport.... more of this in part 2 when we look at influencing.

But seriously though how important is it to you? I'm guessing like everyone else ... super important. Not just for work but for all aspects of life.

If you went to see a doctor and, before they started their diagnosis, you asked, 'just out of interest before you start your doctor stuff, how much do you know about medicine?' and they answered.... 'Oohh ... not much, I've been on a course, googled a few things'... you might be a little concerned as understanding medicine is an essential part of their job.

Hopefully, you get the point, albeit before we have had time to build rapport!

If communication is an essential part of your job/life hopefully this guide will give you a deeper understanding of the subject and inspire you to continue studying this most intriguing area. This guide will provide you with an overview of how communication & influencing work; with lots of practical exercises and techniques immediately applicable and in my experience unbelievably useful. To be clear, this is not a book on the written word. I am dyslexic, blind in one eye and partial to a slight stammer. I don't claim to be a 'writer'. People who attend my sessions and go on to read my guides always tell me 'your books sound like you talking' - Audiobooks next on the agenda!

How important are words in communication?

Spend some time watching how most people communicate and you will observe their weapon of choice is just using words. So, if words are the main way we communicate it begs the question how relevant or important are they in communication?

Exercise

This is one of my favourite exercises to demonstrate the importance of words in communication. It always works, is usually hilarious and proves a significant point.

I tell the group we are going to attempt a quick communication exercise around how we use words.

On the screen, I show two world common words:

- Education

- Love

I explain that wherever you go around the world as long as people speak English everyone will know what these words are. If I'm speaking to a Kazak about love, as long as they speak English they get it.

I get the group to choose which word they would like to use for the exercise, I explain that education always works, and so does love except love is a lot more interesting. I also usually have love in large pink writing and explain we are not going to do anything physical.

They always choose love!
I ask them to write down five words they associate with love and to make sure no one else can see their list. Please feel free to take part by writing down the 5 top words you associate with love.

I then ask for a volunteer who is happy to share their list, I don't force this and suggest if no one volunteers I will use my list of 5 but to bear in mind I may be able to manipulate them! I always get a volunteer. In the past I've used the word sex instead of love, it's a bit riskier and you have an increased chance of no volunteers. I then quickly check the volunteer's 5 words to makes sure it's a list that should be shared with the group, especially if we're using the word sex as some people's list may be career threatening! I once did a conference speech using sex as the word and a sweet old granny decided to share her list, it was very, very rude... some people's inner thinking should remain that way.

We go through the volunteer's list one at a time on a flip chart and I ask the group to raise their hands if they have the same word as the volunteer. It needs to be the same word or the plural of that word and not a different word... as that's a different word! So, what we are looking for is how many matches we have to one of the world's most common words... LOVE... every song has love in it except paperback writer by the Beatles. I know that's not true, I'm just showing off some Beatles trivia, although it must appear in more than 80%+ of songs.

If you want to take part write down the top 5 words you associate with love and I will show you the collective all-time top 5 overleaf. I will also show the top 5 for sex just in case you want to be a bit naughtier!
By the way, rarely do you get more than a 30% match on any word (maybe on one of them) the other 4 words are a 10% match or less. So, no peaking, write down your list of 5.

The top 5

Love

1. Family
2. Their partner's name (shame on you if you have a partner and they are not on your list!)
3. Hate
4. Friends
5. Pets

Sex

1. Passion
2. Fun
3. Pleasure
4. Orgasm
5. Messy

I then ask what does this tell you about communication and words?

They always reply along the lines of 'words don't have any meaning except your perception of that word at that time'.

Communication can be a little tricky as words don't really have any common meaning. People may look like they are talking about the same thing on the surface level as they are using similar words, however in their head they are worlds apart. To add more twists to the plot, human beings are unconscious creatures who spend most of their day on autopilot seeing what they believe and not believing what they see. If you think it can be simplified by the written word you may be mistaken. Take a read of the text overleaf and count the number of Fs

FINISHED FILES ARE THE RES
ULT OF YEARS OF SCIENTI
FIC STUDY COMBINED WITH
THE EXPERIENCE OF YEARS

95% of people get this wrong so don't worry if you didn't see 6. If you got 6 first time congratulations apparently you are a genius and if you think everyone sees 6 show it to your friends and revel in your genius-ness. If I hadn't pointed out there were 6 you would forever believe there were 3, 4 or whatever number you counted. You would see what you believe.

You can find more on human behaviour in my ' **A Guide to Motivation & Resilience'**.

So our communication weapon of choice tends to be words whether written or spoken, however words don't seem to have a common meaning when we speak and we struggle to count letters when we read.

This guide will give you the tools to enhance your communication repertoire as well as equip you with the easiest to apply influencing tool that I have learned in my 50 years in the communication game of life.

The words, how we say it & non-verbal

Have you heard of a chap called Dr Birdwhistell? Most people haven't but they agree he has a fabulous name.

To me, Dr Birdwhistell is the grandfather of communication. He produced a book in 1952 on Kinesics, the study of communication and body. Further work by Mehrabian developed the idea that communication involved more than the words which led to the much-misquoted formula that the relationship between the words, how we say things and what we don't say is:

- 7% words
- 38% How we say things (pitch tone timbre etc)
- 55% Non-verbal (body language)

Mehrabian's work is quoted out of context from his original studies. If the above formula was true when I run training sessions it suggests I could mime for 4 hours and the audience would still get over half of what I'm saying.

Having said this, when you ask people for their experience in life, they will always say there is truth in the above formula. They insist that they read more into the 'how' and the 'non-verbal' than just the words. I agree, and so does Dr Birdwhistell, who estimated 60% was related to how and non-verbal.

Let's give it a little test....

Just the words

Do you get emails?

Have you ever got an email from someone where you thought 'gosh what's up with them?', you give them a call to check, and they say I'm fine! Maybe they had the caps locked on making their tone sound grumpy. With just the words we quite often misread the emotion because we can't see it. This is probably the reason why emojis have become part of everyday life as we spend a lot of time with words on text, WhatsApp etc. With books, we only have the words (usually). Your imagination creates far more than the words can ever achieve.

The words and how we say it

This short, simple sentence has a different meaning when you emphasise different words in the sentence. Try it for yourself, with more volume on the word in bold. The whole message changes.

I didn't say she stole the money.

I didn't **say** she stole the money.

I didn't say **she** stole the money.

Have you been on the phone to someone whom you've never met before, but you're having a discussion resulting in booking a face to face meeting? Do you ever imagine what they will look like based on your conversation?

Have you ever seen your favourite radio DJ in person for the first time? Do they look anything like you thought they would? Back in the day I used to listen to Steve Wright on BBC Radio 1 (UK radio station if you are outside the UK). He had and still does have the most amazing, powerful voice; he was then the main man on the radio. I then saw him for the first time on Top of the Pops (a famous UK music TV show); I almost wrote a letter of complaint to the BBC. This can't be Steve Wright; he looks nothing like his voice, he's all moustached and a bit weasley looking!

Rarely do they look like you imagined. The point is when we just have the words and the 'how we say it', we make up the non-verbal. So be careful how you say things especially if they can't see you, you may be portraying an unintended image. If you spend your day communicating using the telephone (call centres etc.) you might want to make sure your voice makes you sound like you are alive and interested in the other person.

Many years ago I sold advertising over the telephone for Today Newspaper (the first colour newspaper in the UK).

I was given these 3 tips.

1. Smile when you dial - we will touch on this later in the non-verbal language section
2. Stand up when calling - as above
3. Dress for the occasion – looking good feeling good

A few years later, when selling Insurance to Doctors I had to spend a fair amount of time calling potential prospects to try and arrange meetings. I worked from home at the time, and early on slipped into the habit of starting my phone calls in my pyjamas. After a few weeks of mixed results I remembered point 3 from my newspaper training; dress for the occasion. Highly successful executives don't gain their success from hanging around in their PJs all day! How you dress affects your state of mind…. 'looking good, feeling good'. My results got significantly better.

We will dig deeper into points 1 & 2 under the non-verbal language session; the reasons should be pretty obvious. Your mind and body are connected. You energise the body (smile, stand up) and you excite the mind. If your state of mind is improved your communication and influence will be enhanced.

The words the music & the dance

Let's look at all three combined:

- The words
- How we say it
- Non-verbal language

Can you think of a world-famous speech?

The most popular answer by far is 'I have a dream' by Martin Luther King.

The speech is 1,667 words long, over 50 years old and is played every year on its anniversary. How much can you remember? Most people struggle to get past 'I have a dream' and maybe reference to colour and creed and kids playing together.

Maybe that's a tricky speech.

The 2nd most popular when I'm in the UK is anything Winston Churchill related.

'We will fight them on the beaches', 'this was their finest hour', 'never was so much owed by so many to so few'....

His speeches made the country believe we would be alright during troubled times. Can you remember anything other than the above snippets?

We will fight them on the beaches was a long speech, what else can you remember?

If he just said 'we will fight them on the beaches' then dropped the mike and walked off stage we might be a little concerned about the strategy. Just the beaches .... what about some tanks and planes, perhaps the sand dunes Mr Churchill?

The point is we don't remember what people say; we remember whether we get the context, the message and whether we believed them. If you don't believe me try and remember the details from the last speech you heard. You might find it a bit tricky!

Do you give speeches? If so, do you think people will remember what you said? They will remember the overview and context of your message and how congruent your words were combined with how you talked and your non-verbal language.

Public speaking is the number one fear in the world; death is number 3. In general, people would rather die than give a speech. The cruel irony is that people who fear public speaking spend all their time concentrating on the words they will be using rather than the 'how and non-verbal'. I will give you some quick tips on public speaking later on.

Sometimes I like to play with a group when covering this session. I go a little quiet to get their attention and then say something along the lines of the following with my voice in a flat tone, shoulders down, slightly hunched looking a little sour:

'You are without a doubt the finest people I have ever worked with; it's been an absolute joy'.

You get a slightly weird reaction. They smile like you've given a compliment, but there is a look of unease in their faces, you can almost read their minds. 'He said all those nice things but.... I'm not sure it's true'.

The words were ...

'You are without a doubt the finest people I have ever worked with; it's been an absolute joy'.

But if you lessen the how and turn the non-verbal down the impact changes as there is no congruence between the words, how and non-verbal. Whereas if you increase the passion, raise the hands up, lift the shoulders, smile, the whole message changes.

As I write this book the UK is going through political turbulence around BREXIT. You only need to turn on the TV and watch a few politicians to see this lack of congruence between what they say (the words) and what they don't say (the how and non-verbal). Gosh, we are in desperate need of some good leaders that we can believe in!

In summary, when you are communicating with someone or a group, the words need to be relevant to the conversation, however, how you say it and what you say with your body is what will remain with them.

Rapport

Have you noticed that when you are with your friends you start to pick up their mannerisms, use their phrases and even begin to copy their accent? I have a few friends from Liverpool, when I spend time with them I get a little bit Scouser; when in Cardiff (capital of South Wales ... my homeland) I get a bit Cardiff like!

When we are with people we like we tend to be like them. It's called rapport. Rapport is a deep level of understanding and connection with another person. When in this state communication is easy, it's like a flow state, a sixth sense.

When our words, how & non-verbal are similar to another person we are more likely to achieve rapport. Next time you are out with a group of friends having a lovely time you may notice you are all sitting in a similar way, you all know when it's time to leave, you seem synchronised.

Have you ever had a good meeting?

Have you ever had a bad meeting?

If you had a magic video camera that could play back each one, the chances are in the good meeting you are very much aligned in the words, how and non-verbal; in the bad, different in every way, especially the non-verbal.

I spend a lot of my time away from home working in London. I quite like to go to the pub and watch people... not in a creepy way, although as I type this it sounds a bit creepy! Whilst you can't hear most people's conversation, you can get a good idea of how it's going by what they are saying with their body. If they look similar, in tune, mimicking, all is well. Out of tune, out of sync, slap around the face... not so good.

Lots of offices these days have clear glass meeting rooms (you can see in). You can tell how a meeting is going just by how people are sitting. If similar body language, probably good, if very different, probably not so good.

When in rapport we naturally tend to mirror the person we are with. When in rapport you are more likely to have influence with the person you are with.

The next two chapters will dive deeper into the how and the non-verbal, to give you some insight into how you might want to change your approach to help gain rapport when your communication isn't working.

How we say it

The first thing here is to state the obvious. Make sure how you put your message across is congruent with the attitude you want to display.

If you want to appear passionate about something... sound passionate.

If you want to appear happy... sound happy.

You must have come across people who are trying to communicate a positive message and look like they are chewing a wasp, or upbeat with the face of a mortician. People won't believe you unless how you say it matches the mood you are trying to portray.

A little tip...

If you are unsure how to sound happy, think back to the last time you were deliriously happy and daydream the memory. That's what it will sound like! (More of this when we look at preparation for influencing).

So, decide the pace, timbre, tone, volume etc. to match the attitude you are attempting to portray.

The area I want to cover in this section on 'How we say it' relates to 3 of your five senses.

The five senses are:

Sight (Visual)
Sound (Auditory)
Touch/feel (Kinaesthetic)
Taste (Gustatory)
Smell (Olfactory)

Are you aware when we communicate we talk in pictures (visual), sounds (auditory) and feelings/touch/do (kinaesthetic)?

We switch between each of the senses, sometimes we might be in auditory mode, other times kinaesthetic etc. More often than not we have a preference for some over the others. For example, I'm more kinaesthetic & visual than auditory. My preference for communication is for you to show me (visual) then allow me to draw all over it (kinaesthetic). If you just talk to me I shut down very quickly.

We also communicate through the other two, olfactory (smell) and gustatory (taste) however, I've yet to find a practical way to use them in a business or personal context. It's considered a bit weird to sniff people as they walk into a room or give them a damn good licking!

So back to the three: Visual, kinaesthetic & auditory - VKA for short.

If someone says to you in conversation 'show me what you mean' what do you think most people do? Most talk to the other person about what they mean, they use auditory. However, the person has asked for a visual representation 'show me what you mean'. It might be an idea to draw them something.

People give clues in what they want by how they speak.

Tell me how that works – A
Show me what you mean - V
That feels a little rough to me - K (feel/touch/do)

You could really get into this subject and analyse exactly what people say and adapt your language to suit what mode people are in. If they are in auditory mode, use auditory language, if visual use visual language etc. People like people who are like them, so in theory, if you use their mode of language they will feel a deeper level of rapport.

Personally, I find this beyond my brain capacity to do naturally. I have seen many people carry out this style of mimicking the VKA modes and frankly they sound odd. I'm sure there are Jedi Knights out there using their powers of VKA mode switching to influence the fu*k out of people but, as they are so good, I guess I haven't noticed.

I like to keep things simple. If you know roughly what the general population's preference is, then as long as you cover that you should be alright.

Teachers in schools know all about this. When I went to Primary school (kids below age 10) my classroom was barren, dull, black and white. That was 40 years ago! My children's classrooms when they were that age were very different; full of colour, visuals, sounds, tactile experiences, a wonderland for the senses. We learn through our senses, schools know this, we communicate through our senses, a lot of adults don't realise this!

When I am running a communication and influencing course I get delegates to complete a Visual, Kinaesthetic, Auditory preference survey so they can gauge how they prefer to take in information. I must have done this over a thousand times. The results are pretty consistent.

The percentage order of VKA highest scores are:

60% have Visual as first
40% have Kinaesthetic as first
0-10% have Auditory as first

80% have the combination of V&K first and second (either way around).
Auditory is rarely scored high and is usually a distant 3rd place.

How much % time do we spend talking compared to showing and doing?
The message is clear - Show (Visual), get them involved (Kinaesthetic) and also talk (Auditory). Stop relying on just Auditory.

Don't take my word for it, take the test. Afterwards, I'll show you how this can help your love life, become a world-famous leader (if that's your desire) and aid presentations.

Overleaf is the start of a short VKA quiz that will give you a guide to your general preference.

VKA quiz

Please circle the response that most appeals to you.

1. When I operate new equipment I generally:
   a) read the instructions first
   b) listen to an explanation from someone who has used it before
   c) go ahead and have a go, I can figure it out as I use it

2. When I need directions for travelling I usually:
   a) look at a map
   b) ask for spoken directions
   c) follow my nose and maybe use a compass

3. When I cook a new dish I like to:
   a) follow a written recipe
   b) call a friend for an explanation
   c) follow my instincts, tcsting as I cook

4. If I am teaching someone something new I tend to:
   a) Draw it for them, or write instructions
   b) give them a verbal explanation
   c) demonstrate first and then let them have a go

5. I tend to say:
   a) watch how I do it
   b) listen to me explain
   c) you have a go

6. During my free time I most enjoy:
   a) going to museums and galleries
   b) listening to music and talking to my friends
   c) playing sport or doing DIY

7. When I go shopping for clothes I tend to:
   a)   imagine what they would look like on
   b)   discuss them with the shop staff
   c)   try them on and test them out

8. When I am choosing a holiday I usually:
   a)   read lots of brochures
   b)   listen to recommendations from friends
   c)   imagine what it would be like to be there

9. If I was buying a new car I would:
   a)   read reviews in newspapers and magazines
   b)   discuss what I need with my friends
   c)   test-drive lots of different types

10. When I am learning a new skill I am most comfortable:
   a)   watching what the teacher is doing
   b)   talking through with the teacher exactly what I'm supposed to do
   c)   giving it a try myself and working it out as I go

11. If I am choosing food from a menu I tend to:
   a)   imagine what the food will look like
   b)   talk through the options in my head or with my partner
   c)   imagine what the food will taste like

12. When I listen to a band I can't help:
   a)   watching the band members and other people in the audience
   b)   listening to the lyrics and the beats
   c)   moving in time with the music

13. When I concentrate I most often:
    a) focus on the words or the pictures in front of me
    b) discuss the problem and the possible solutions in my head
    c) move around a lot, fiddle with pens and pencils and touch things

14. I choose household furnishings because I like:
    a) their colours and how they look
    b) the descriptions the salespeople give me
    c) their textures and what it feels like to touch them

15. My first memory is of:
    a) looking at something
    b) being spoken to
    c) doing something

16. When I am anxious I:
    a) visualise the worst-case scenarios
    b) talk over in my head what worries me most
    c) can't sit still, fiddle and move around constantly

17. I feel especially connected to other people because of:
    a) how they look
    b) what they say to me
    c) how they make me feel

18. When I have to revise for an exam I generally:
    a) write lots of revision notes and diagrams
    b) talk over my notes, alone or with other people
    c) imagine creating the formula

19. If I am explaining something to someone I tend to:
    a)   show them what I mean
    b)   explain to them in different ways until they understand
    c)   encourage them to try and talk them through my idea as they do it

20. I really love:
    a)   watching films, photography, looking at art or people watching
    b)   listening to music, the radio or talking to friends
    c)   taking part in sporting activities, eating fine foods and wines or dancing

21. Most of my free time is spent:
    a)   watching television
    b)   talking to friends
    c)   doing physical activity or making things

22. When I first contact a new person I usually:
    a)   arrange a face to face meeting
    b)   talk to them on the telephone
    c)   try to get together whilst doing something else, such as an activity or a meal

23. I first notice how people:
    a)   look and dress
    b)   sound and speak
    c)   stand and move

24. If I am angry I tend to:
    a) keep replaying in my mind what it is that has upset me
    b) raise my voice and tell people how I feel
    c) stamp about, slam doors and physically demonstrate my anger

25. I find it easiest to remember:
    a) faces
    b) names
    c) things I have done

26. I think that you can tell someone is lying if:
    a) they avoid looking at you
    b) their voice changes
    c) they give you funny vibes

27. When I meet an old friend:
    a) I say 'it's great to see you!'
    b) I say 'it's great to hear from you!'
    c) I give them a hug or a handshake

28. I remember things best by:
    a) writing notes or keeping printed details
    b) saying them aloud or repeating words and key points in my head
    c) doing and practising the activity or imagining it being done

29. If I have to complain about faulty goods, I am most comfortable:
    a) writing an email
    b) complaining over the phone
    c) taking the item back to the store or posting it to head office

30. I tend to say:
   a) I see what you mean
   b) I hear what you are saying
   c) I know how you feel

Now add up how many As, Bs and Cs you selected.

As =   Bs =   Cs =

If you chose mostly As you have a **VISUAL** preference.

If you chose mostly Bs you have an **AUDITORY** preference.

If you chose mostly Cs you have a **KINAESTHETIC** preference.

It's common to have two strong scores and one weaker. Some people find their preference is a balanced blend of all three.

Let me guess, a higher V or K score over A? If you are one of the few who have a higher auditory score, compare with some friends so you can see if my % breakdown of more people with V&K stands up to scrutiny. Often those with a high Auditory have some background in music and (or given the affordability) spend a decent amount on the quality of their hifi system. The quality of the sound is important to them.

Let's examine this at a very high level, then bring it down to your love life and hopefully settle on the principle - if you can, show (visual) and get them to do (kinaesthetic) when you communicate.

Becoming a world-famous leader!

Let's start at a high level and see how to become a world-famous leader who stays in people's memory for a long time.

This is the theory: If you wanted to be a world-famous leader who leaves a legacy then if you look right or distinctive (V), sound right (A) and connect with people on an emotional level (K), you will tap into the preference of everyone in the voting population. This assumes that the majority of people don't really have a passion, interest or deep understanding of politics. Some do, but a large majority haven't got a Scooby Do. So, if you are very visual you will have a leaning toward someone who looks right, if Kinaesthetic a leaning to someone who connects with you emotionally. So, if you can tick all the boxes then you will connect at a deep level with most people. I usually do this live in a training session and get the delegates to shout out names of world-famous leaders (good or bad) who we will remember for a long time and then a list of those we will forget easily.

The rememberable (not a real word but I think it should be):

JFK
Churchill
Mandela
Obama
Hitler
Gandhi
Mrs Thatcher
Donald Trump!!

Visual - will you always remember them? - probably yes

Auditory - either awesome voices or very memorable (Trump, Mrs T)

Kinaesthetic - did they stir people's emotions - absolutely. Donald and Mrs T fall into the camp of you either love them or hate them.

Donald rode a wave of emotion and backlash against the Clinton empire. You will never forget how he looks and sounds... he certainly stirs your emotions!

Those we will forget

Not surprisingly delegates struggle a bit to remember these people, so I take them back to the last two elections in the UK:

Ed Miliband
Dave Cameron
Nick Clegg
Mrs May
Jeremy Corbyn

Nick and Dave looked more like a Prime Minister than Ed. Nick messed up when he went back on his promise to the students, which left Dave looking, sounding, and feeling more like a Prime Minister. Ed falling off stages, struggling to eat a bacon sandwich, and acting weirdly tough had a negative impact on all aspects of VKA. Dave won. Did you notice that Jeremy upgraded his suits after his last election loss in 2017 (smart dark blue ones)!

I did this exercise the day before Obama won against McCain. At the time it was a tight race. The delegates predicted Obama to win based on VKA.

Tony Blair ticked all the boxes when he got elected, he was young, fresh ... it was 'Cool Britannia'. Post Iraq war he looked haunted, a shadow of his former self... his VKA powers had dwindled. I don't think hanging out with George Bush jnr helped, Blair never managed to carry off the denim cowboy boots look!

This is a scary thought... Boris Johnson!!! Very distinctive look, voice and definitely stirs emotions. Look out Great Britain! (I wrote this before he became PM. I've left it in for posterity).

So... if you want to be a world-famous leader who people remember, make sure you look, sound and feel right.

Your love life

Bringing this all down to a lower level, let's apply it to your love life.

The theory here is that for us to feel truly loved we need one of the VKA to be fulfilled above all others. For me I need my wife to provide me with a kinaesthetic experience... it's not rude, I just need her to hold my hand when we go for a walk, if she does, I know she loves me even though I'm not sure she wants to hold my hand as I'm quite a hot person (temperature).

Do you remember when you met your first 'special' person? Life feels so good, you have butterflies in your stomach, stay up all night talking, skip on the way to work, whistle, and smile for no reason. This is the honeymoon period, way before any honeymoon. What happens after a period of time? Life goes back to normal and you stop skipping or smiling for no reason on the way to work.

When we first meet that special person we fire off on all of the 5 senses:

Bunch of flowers (V)
I love you (A)
Kiss kiss hug hug (K).

(again we will ignore olfactory and gustatory ...eeewww ☹)

So, whatever our new partner's preference we will definitely connect with their most important driver. Then after a while the relationship matures and settles down, and sometimes unfortunately deteriorates. There could be many reasons for this, one of the theories is a mismatch in VKA can signal trouble as deep down if you don't feel loved because you are kinaesthetic and your partner doesn't do kinaesthetic you won't feel loved... and you won't know why!!

For example:

- A Kinaesthetic partner approaching a Visual partner wanting a hug, the Visual partner might be thinking or saying 'back off me, I'm not a piece of meat... buy me something'.
- A Visual partner buys a gift for an Auditory partner.... 'you can't buy me; just tell me you love me'.

If you are in a relationship try all 3 and see which gets you the best reaction, or if it's not too weird get them to complete the questionnaire and have a discussion around preferences and love.

My preference order is K with a very close V score and hardly any A. If you talk to me, I shut down very quickly. If you draw it (V) and let me interact and draw as well (K), I get it. Anybody who has been coached by me will probably notice I'm drawing all the time to demonstrate.

My kinaesthetic preference comes out in how I look and buy things. I could buy a new suit and within an hour look like I've slept on a station. Kinaesthetic people tend to have a 'lived in' comfortable look, Visual people look well put together.... I'm not really sure what Auditory people look like! When I buy clothes the feel is more important than the look, I struggle to buy online unless I have brought it previously (I know what it will feel like). I can't bear the touch of polystyrene, I feel uncomfortable with salty beach hands, a sofa's comfort level is more important than the look, and so on.

MMIs - Use in presentations

I used to give presentations to doctors on financial planning. We made sure our visuals looked professional and interesting (V), made sure our voices sounded confident & passionate (A) and we achieved good results (doctors wanted to use our services). When we added
Kinaesthetic into the presentation the results went from good to awesome. We achieved this by giving

the doctors a template of a financial graph for life which they completed (kinaesthetic) during the presentation. This way they took part in a very visual and kinaesthetic way. A few years ago I went on a magic course for a day, it was fabulous and I learnt a few tricks, however the most amazing thing I learnt was to build in MMIs into a presentation. MMIs stand for Magical Moments of Insight, Interest & Interaction. The Interaction part of MMIs is a very strong demonstration of kinaesthetic (K). When I build a presentation I check the number of MMIs to make sure the presentation has kinaesthetic engagement. Remember, if you give presentations the audience won't really remember what was said, they will get the context and how it made them feel. If you can show them and engage them through MMIs your presentations will be loved.

If you are one of those people that presents in a solely auditory fashion, which is just having bullet point words on the screen and then talking the audience through exactly what is on the screen.... stop it, you are killing people.

Key point on VKA in communication:

Auditory seems to be the main tool that most people use when communicating which is against their own and others' preferences. If given the opportunity I would suggest you consider how to show and get them to do!

Non-verbal language (body language)

'No, I'm never gonna dance again, guilty feet
no rhythm'. George Michael Careless whispe

What's the most honest part of body language
George Michael was way ahead of his time in ma
ways. Apparently, your feet. You can't dance with
your partner if you are cheating on them.

Body language is such a fascinating subject. As this is
a guide, I plan to outline the mechanics and let you
observe them in real life. I will recommend my
favourite book on the subject by an ex-FBI agent at
the end of this section.

The first thing to mention here is it is all very well
understanding how to read others' body language but
in a way a bit pointless if you don't observe the
signals you give off with yours. You may not realise
the stinky message you send with your non-verbal
cues.

Many years ago I ran a full week course on selling;
believe it or not 20 years ago we had time to take a
whole week off to attend a course! Anyway, at the
back of the course sat a good friend of mine, who
spent the whole week looking like he was chewing a
wasp (not a friendly look). At the end of the week I
caught up with him and said, 'Gus I really need to
have a chat; I think I need to resign on Monday as
that must have been a stinker of a course... you
looked so miserable'.

He replied, 'no way mate, that was the best course
I've ever been on... that's my concentration face'.

′s commonly referred to as the resting bitch

ʒo through this section reflect on how you
ıg across as well as how you read others.
.y be sending all the wrong signals, which, in
 rong company may be career threatening
 ıthout a word being said. More about the feet soon
 ıut let's start with a simple approach.

Matching or mirroring

If you're having a conversation with someone and
your message isn't getting through, do you try and
put it across in a different way? If you don't, give it a
go as continuing to do the same thing and expecting a
different result is like banging your head against a
brick wall and wondering why your head hurts.

If you do try putting your message across in a
different way (the how), can I also suggest you
consider putting your body across in a different way
as well (non-verbal). When we get on well with
someone, how we say it, and what we don't say (non-
verbal) are usually quite aligned. So, if you would
change the how, why not change the body to align
with the other person. Just be a bit subtle!! If they
scratch their nose don't suddenly scratch yours, if
they put their hands on their heads don't suddenly do
the same. You will look like a mimicking clown.
When people talk, they tend to shut down their
observations of the world, so when they are talking sit
a bit like them. This is called matching (the same) or
mirroring (mirror image). You can try this at many
levels. You can match their words, their breathing (a
little bit seductive) and their body posture.

Personally, I don't think too hard about this and naturally adopt a similar posture, I've done it for so many years I don't actually consciously think about doing it, I just do it.

Like any theory there is lots of debate about whether matching or mirroring works. I think it does as long as you are natural and have a genuine interest in the other person. If you are unsure, I would suggest you observe it for a few weeks, watch people together, observe the interaction of your friends and see whether they are matching and mirroring naturally. If you decide to do it, as stated previously, be a little subtle, and don't worry about being found out 'excuse me are you copying my body language'? I have done this for twenty plus years and had it done to me probably thousands of times and I can only really remember one person who I noticed deliberately doing it. His name was Ed from Birmingham. Any time 1 did something he copied me, so I played with him and started doing weird body movements to see if he would follow. he did! As long as you are subtle no one will notice, you will feel very conscious at first but after practicing it will become unconscious (autopilot).

Matching and mirroring is usually day 2 or 3 of any sales training course, it's in many ways the simplest approach to body language. Just be a bit like the other person. To use the old adage; people like people who are like them.

Are you too close?

Everybody has had the experience of being with someone who gets too close, the space invaders. For most we find this a very unpleasant experience and certainly a rapport breaker. Have you ever been at a social event when a person gets too close so you step back, then they step forward so you end up stepping back, and so on like you are doing some weird backward conga? We are too polite to say something. 'Hey back off, you're way too close'. If we don't tell people, how do you know it's not you, that you're not a space invader? Well you may answer 'because I am self-aware'. I may point out, 'if space invaders had self-awareness they wouldn't step forward every time someone stepped back'... it could be you!!

Here is a little tip:

When meeting someone step in and greet (handshake, kiss on cheek etc), then take one step back and see what they do. If they stay where they are, you are the perfect distance from them. If they step back, you are too close. If they step forward, you have a space invader on your hands. Unfortunately if you want rapport you will have to grin and bear it.

General guide - 4 levels of distance control

These are guides rather than rules, culture, family, background will have an impact.

Level: 4 Social (3 or 4ft to 12ft)

If someone enters the radius of around 12ft your unconscious is alert to the fact they may want a conversation.

When training a group of people I get half to stand on one side of the room facing the other half so they are opposite a partner. I then get one side to walk toward the other side (in a non-creepy way) and stop when they reach the right distance for a social chat. They stop around 3 to 4ft (unless you have a space invader who gets closer!). I then ask the group to take one more step toward their partner, and you see the immediate non-verbal clues of deep discomfort in the partner; they are too close. The same applies if you walk up behind someone, 3 to 4ft is OK, any closer causes the hairs on the back of your neck to rise.

So you can have a social chat from 3 to 4ft up to around 12ft apart.

Level 3: Personal (18 inches to 3 to 4ft)

Reserved for close friends who you trust, partner and family

Level 2: Intimate (6 to 18 inches)

Partner and family

Level 1: Close intimate (0-6 inches)

Partner... maybe your dog

Reading non-verbal signals

I'll reference my favourite book on this subject at the end of this section. My kids have read it; I remember one of them coming back from school saying, 'I think my teacher was telling fibs today'.

Why was George Michael so ahead of his time with his reference to guilty feet?

The limbic brain system is in charge of your body language. It's on 24 hours a day and keeps you alive from predator attacks. Most of the time humans operate on autopilot, like when you drive a car and wonder how you arrived at your destination. Once you know how to do something you work on autopilot. When faced with danger the autopilot system brings the limbic brain in to deal with it. If you are being attacked by a tiger, oxygen is directed towards the limbic brain system, cortisol, testosterone released, bowels are emptied to lighten the load etc. You will visibly see someone's body change as the limbic brain takes charge. When a social threat occurs the autopilot brain sends a similar message to the limbic brain. Whilst we don't usually poop ourselves under social threat we will get chemical changes in the body as well as changes in our body language. The rational thinking brain comes in after the limbic brain has dealt with the short-term emergency.

Example

Swimming minding your own business – autopilot

See a shark. - Limbic brain takes charge in this order:

Freeze - so the shark doesn't notice you

Flight - swim away the fastest you have ever swum once it sees you

Fight - bash it on the nose when at last chance saloon.

When safely ashore the rational brain pops in to say hello and reasons that swimming in shark infested waters was not a good idea. Once you enter the water you enter the food chain!

My personal view is that it's very difficult to be exact in reading body language, however if you understand what's driving it, you should pick up enough clues as to whether you've receiving a positive or negative signal. As the limbic brain comes into play before the rational brain, you will get leakage of someone's reaction before they get to adjust their position and say what they rationally think is the right thing to say.

I'm not sure you will be able to read minds after spending some time developing your non-verbal reading skills, however you should be able to gauge whether what you are saying is having a positive or negative impact. Also, it will give you some clues as to what messages you're sending with your own non-verbals. It may be wise to change your body posture if, when speaking to your boss your non-verbals give off the message 'I think you are an arse'.

The limbic brain works in the following way when dealing with threat:

Freeze
Flight
Fight

My little shark story before followed this order. Back in the day when we were surrounded by things that could eat us we would freeze if we saw a predator, try and stay small, not move. If the predator saw us, we would run (flight), the predator would usually work on a chase, trip and bite mechanism. If cornered, we would have no choice but to fight.

So, when you are observing body language bear in mind what the limbic brain does - Freeze, Flight or Fight.

The feet are a very honest part of body language (some would argue the most honest) because you need them for freeze flight or fight. When freezing we need a stable platform, we run with our feet and, if you watch any drunken men getting aggressive, they start fighting with their feet.

The following is a high-level guide to body language.

Baseline behaviour

First things first. When observing someone's body language note their baseline behaviour i.e. what do they normally do. So, if someone normally crosses their arms that's baseline and don't read anything into it other than it's normal. If they don't normally cross their arms and after you've said something, they do.... then you may be receiving a negative clue from their limbic brain. If you get a cluster of signals you can increase your certainty. So, if they cross arms, flare their nasals, raise one eyebrow, go red and then call you a dick... you have some clear signals!

A quick tour of the body from feet to eyes:

Feet

Often referred to as the most honest part of body language as first to come into play when we freeze, flight or fight. Also we have never been told to watch our feet, we have always been told to watch our face... 'smile at scary Aunty Doris and pretend you like her'.

Feet point towards what they like and where they want to go if they are not happy. If you are having a meeting with someone and their feet start pointing towards the door, that's probably where they want to go. If you try and feed your baby and they've had enough the feet will start pointing away from you. If you are standing in a circle of friends, it's likely the most popular person will have the most feet pointing toward them. As mentioned earlier in the book I spend a lot of time away from home working in London. In the evening I like to go to a pub and watch people... in a non–creepy way!! If a couple have their feet pointing into each other, chances are they are into each other. If one of the couple's feet start pointing toward the rather attractive person across the bar, then maybe that's where they want to be.

If you see two people standing with one ankle crossing the other, do you think this is a good or bad sign?

If you think back to the limbic brain it would never let you stand next to someone like this if you thought there was threat as you couldn't freeze, flight or fight in this position. You are likely to be very comfortable with the person you are with, or very subservient.

Policemen or Bouncers stand with legs apart, they are not freezing (they are very visible), certainly not in flight, definitely ready for a fight. Alpha type people in business meetings occupy a lot of space, they spread their stuff out. I'm not freezing, or flighting, I'm in charge.
Teenage boys occupy a large space on a sofa with that arrogant teenage look. 'Yeh Dad whatever'.
Interestingly if you invade their space and sit close to them without saying a word they lose their power.

'What Dad, what... you're weird'.

Up and down

Anything that grips us to planet earth is usually a bad sign, anything that lifts us up is usually a good sign. Up probably good, down not so good.

Thumbs up = good, thumbs down not so good.
Smokers in a good mood smoke up, slightly pensive down.
Jumping up in the air, good. Holding onto a chair when in a meeting, not so good.
A smile is up :), frown is down:(

When you have a dodgy plane landing everyone is gripping the seat :(when you land safely arms raised... yeeha :)

So, if you are having a meeting with someone and they start gripping the chair to hold onto planet earth... not so good.

Arms crossed

Remember baseline behaviour. A lot of people sit with arms crossed because they find it comfortable or because they are cold.

If it's not their norm, it's likely to be a negative signal as crossing the body protects the major organs. It's why we feel uncomfortable when people who we don't know intimately get too close. If you happen to be on the London Underground it's horrible when someone is in your face or up close and personal behind as you have no protection. It's a little more bearable if they are to your side as you have protection from your flanks.

Arms open suggests a positive mood. We leave ourselves physically vulnerable suggesting comfort in what is happening. Open body = happy mind. Closed body = closed mind.

So, if you sit in meetings with your arms crossed with a resting bitch face, don't be surprised if people misread you.

Touching of the neck, face

This is usually a sign of someone pacifying themselves.

When I'm coaching I can tell when someone is getting a little uncomfortable about a commitment to do something when they start rubbing the back of their neck. They may be saying 'yes I'm committed to doing that', but the body is saying 'no chance' or 'this is really scary'. I ask some more questions to try and really understand how they are feeling.

Pupil dilation

Good or bad??

Pupils dilate to let more light in because they are attracted to what they see or in fear and need to see more. Zombies have enlarged pupils to scare the unconscious daylights out of us. Reading people's pupil dilation can be a little tricky unless they have crystal clear blue eyes. You tend to break rapport if you step in too close and stare at someone's pupils. I remember reading about research on how powerful pupil dilation works on an unconscious level. The research was along these lines: A very attractive model had her face photographed. Two groups of men were asked to view her photograph and rate how beautiful she was. The first group had the normal photo, the second had the same photo except it was photoshopped to enlarge her pupils. The second group rated her far more beautiful than the first even though it was the same photo with a minor change that wouldn't be visible to the conscious mind.

Pupil dilation could also just mean the person is on drugs. So, attraction, deep fear or drugs … take your choice!

Eye movements

I first read about this many years ago, gosh it got me excited especially as I was told it was an old KGB, CIA technique. Again, like any theory always at risk of being debunked. For me like most things try it for yourself and see if it works (If you read a lot of detective crime thrillers no doubt you will have noticed eye movements being referenced).

In the 80s we were told to have strong eye contact. This is of course nonsense and damn weird. If someone speaks to you with laser like eye contact, it will frighten the life out of you. When we talk it's natural for our eyes to go all over the place. When you listen its good practice to have good eye contact as it shows you are engaged. In addition, when shaking someone's hand it's good to initially have eye contact, just don't keep staring at them!

The theory is that your eyes go in different directions depending on whether you are going to the past, future, visual, auditory, kinaesthetic or talking to yourself.

Generally, for a right-handed person the past is on the left (as you look through your own eyes) and the future on the right. Left-handed people tend to be reversed (past on right, future on left).

Visual past is top left, Visual future top right
Auditory past midline left, Auditory future midline right
Kinaesthetic down to the right
Talking to yourself down to the left (auditory digital)
Again, all from the perspective of looking through your own eyes

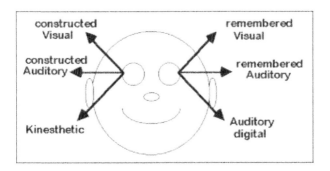

constructed Visual — remembered Visual
constructed Auditory — remembered Auditory
Kinesthetic — Auditory digital

Here is where the KGB and CIA reference comes in:

If you ask someone about something visual relating from the past and they are right-handed you would expect their eyes to go up to the left as they remember. If, however they go up to the right, it would suggest they are constructing something (visual future) rather than remembering something. Have you ever seen someone being interviewed on TV about a murder and the next day getting arrested? I'm guessing the detectives saw something in their body language/eye movements that didn't look right.

I'm not 100% sure whether it is an FBI/CIA technique, but it got me interested.

Test it for yourself. Most people have a strong preference for visual as per VKA chapter. When you are with your mates ask questions about the past and see where their eyes go.
'What did you do on the weekend'? for example. The eyes generally go in a certain direction; top left (through their eyes). When your friends talk about something emotional watch to see if their eyes go down to the right, when they talk to themselves down

to the left (through their eyes for a right-handed person).

I wouldn't use this on your partner as they may become paranoid. They may start wearing shades!

Ice cream or poop?
We move towards things we like (ice cream) and move away from things we don't like (poop).

If somebody leans towards you when you are talking, there is a good chance they like what you are saying. If they move away you've pooped on the table.

If someone says something and then moves away, they've pooped on the table and are distancing themselves from what they've said.

General guide for body language:

- Look for clusters of body language signals – one off signals may just be habit/comfort
- Generally anything that defies gravity is a positive mood
- The feet are possibly the most honest part of the body, they point towards things they like and away if they dislike
- Our bodies are open to things we like and closed to things we dislike
- Neck touching especially signals discomfort
- Any blocking (arms crossed etc) can signal discomfort/dislike
- We are taught to lie with our face
- Trust your gut instinct, you are picking up on some subtle clues

I've read many books on non-verbal language, I find the subject fascinating. My favourite by far and I think the easiest to understand is 'what every body is saying' by Joe Navarro ex FBI agent.

Why not just take a part of the body for a few days at a time to see what you can see. Start with the feet, although don't peak beneath tables at meetings as it gives the wrong impression. Then look at hands, then eye movements, then touching and so on until it all becomes a bit autopilot. We are experts at reading body language I think we've just forgotten what to look out for. When you get that gut feeling about what someone is saying, investigate it as your unconscious mind has probably picked up a non-verbal signal.

Non-verbal exercise

A great exercise to demonstrate the power of non-verbal language when communicating.

Let's say you have 10 people in a room and you want to run a training exercise.

Split them into two groups. If you can, select the chattier people for Group 1.

Explain to the whole group that you want to demonstrate what passion in communication looks like. Ask Group 1 (the chattier group) to stay in the room for instructions and Group 2 to leave the room and wait outside for further instructions once you have prepped Group 1.

Instructions for Group 1

Tell them you want them to demonstrate passion in communication by talking to an individual from Group 2 about a subject they feel passionate about (football, gardening, music... whatever floats their boat) for 30/60 seconds. They need to be passionate but needn't feel self-conscious as there will be a lot of noise in the room with their other colleagues doing the same thing. Tell them they have two minutes to prepare their subject of passion while you go and brief the other group on how looking interested in someone's conversation can be demonstrated. The reason for selecting chattier people for Group 1 is that extraverts tend to find it easier to talk at will!

for Group 2

u have asked Group 1 to talk to
in Group 2 about something they feel
passionate about. When Group 2 go back into the
room they are to pair up with an individual from
Group 1 and, when I give the instruction, to start
looking very interested in what the other person is
saying... good eye contact, good engaging posture,
smiling etc.

They are to look interested until I give a signal,
usually a few coughs (or if they don't hear the cough
due to volume in the room after 10/15 seconds), to
disengage with their body from the conversation.
This could be looking over someone's shoulder,
checking their phone for messages, yawning, turning
away, dropping their shoulders. They don't verbally
disagree, just non-verbal disengagement. I let this
run for 10-20 seconds ...it becomes painful to watch!

I then say 'stop'. The room is usually full of laughter,
chat and energy.

I explain to everyone the instructions I gave to Group
2 (to come in, partner up and initially look interested
in what they were saying). I ask Group 1 'did you
notice Group 2 looking interested at the beginning'?
Most people from Group 1 do notice. If anyone in
Group 2 was found to look disinterested I give some
advice that maybe they should work on their looking
interested skills! Trust me lots of people need to work
on this!

I then apologise for the slight trickery and tell them
Group 2 were asked to disengage with their body

when I coughed (or if they didn't hear me after 10/15 seconds).

I ask Group 1 'did you notice something happened in the conversation when this occurred'?

A resounding 'Yes'.

'How did it make you feel, how did you react'?

When the non-verbal disengagement occurs, the talkers from Group 1 do some of the following things:

- Speed up and talk louder to try and catch their attention
- Lose their passion and energy due to the disengagement
- Get annoyed with the other person
- Think they are boring the other person
- Sometimes because they are so in the flow, and perhaps aren't good readers of people are oblivious to the disengagement.

It's a very blunt way to demonstrate a subtle point.

Have you ever checked your phone when talking to someone, or looked over their shoulder, or tapped away at your laptop as they speak to you, or checked your watch? Most of us have. If you have, you are doing the same thing as the above exercise. You break rapport. If that was your intention well done, if it's not and you want to influence people, give them your full attention non-verbally as well as verbally. When you look over someone's shoulder you could be sending a message that someone or something over there is more interesting than you. Checking your watch could send a signal I need to be somewhere else.

This non-verbal disengagement is becoming a bigger issue as the generations collide.
The Z generation (born with a mobile phone in their hand) find themselves bumping into the X generation (me) who got their first mobile phone around age 25. One set is conditioned to look at a screen (Z gen), the other set conditioned to check their watch (as a kid X gens had to be home at a certain time … no mobile phones). If your boss is an X gen they may judge you as being rude for looking at your phone when in conversation.

As previously discussed on page 32 the limbic system works on ice cream or poop, it moves towards what it likes and away from what it doesn't. The same principle applies when assessing friend or foe. If friend you will be more relaxed, if foe or unsure you will be on guard. If you want to influence someone your chance of success will be increased if they don't consider you a foe. If you build rapport with someone you will more likely be viewed as friend and not foe. Engaging 'non-verbally' and with the 'how you say it' increases rapport and therefore increases your chance of influence.

You could of course have huge influence over someone if they view you as a foe if you have power over them, perhaps a dictator, a bully boss… a bit of a dick! I'm more for the 'win/win' strategy when you look at influence, I'm a bit of a hippy, I think if you go around crapping on people it may come back to bite you. Don't get me wrong, there are plenty of successful people out there with a 'I win/you lose' strategy… they are just not for me.

Part 2 Influencing

Without doubt, this little influencing technique I'm going to share with you next is the most useful thing I've ever learnt in my working and personal life. It is the easiest concept to understand and apply immediately. The only difficulty is that you are an autopilot human being who tends to do things in a conditioned way. To use this technique will probably mean breaking old habits and forming new ones.

To be honest my biggest concern in writing about it is how few pages it will take to explain it, I worry you might feel short changed 'this book cost me the price of a cup of coffee, I expect more than 5 pages'. If you feel that way, I'm more than happy to buy you a coffee if we meet. If it took pages upon pages to explain it, it wouldn't be the easiest concept to understand and apply would it?

Physical demonstration

If you got into a physical pushing competition with someone else there would probably be 3 results:

1. They are stronger than you and they push you over
2. You are stronger than them and you push them over
3. You are of equal strength and spend a lot of time sweating with no movement... a war of attrition

If someone is stronger than you and they push you, if you decided not to push back (natural reaction) but to pull them you could use their body weight and throw them over your shoulder. I've seen enough martial arts films to know there is truth in this....

actually, I've only seen Enter the Dragon and a few Jackie Chan movies but I've worked with lots of martial arts enthusiasts who back me up. The power is in Pull not Push.

The same thing also applies in conversation:

When you Push someone in conversation you put across your point of view, whether that's assertive, persuasive, tentative, shouty, aggressive .... it's your point of view.

When you Pull someone in conversation you are not pushing a point across you are asking questions and listening to gain understanding, you are open to new ideas and ways of doing things. You try to establish common ground and gain rapport with someone.

When you Push someone in conversation you are likely to cause the other person's body to react; chemicals will change, they are likely to release cortisol (stress drug). When you Pull someone in conversation because you are showing interest you are more likely to release oxytocin in the other person... the love drug! Pulling is likely to cause a positive chemical reaction in the other person. Pushing is likely to cause a negative chemical reaction.

I think we are all experts at Pull in our junior years, always enquiring and asking questions, then in the teenage years start Pushing more and more. What's the balance of Push and Pull in your work meetings, the response on average is 70/80% Push with less Pull.

Mostly it's 'I think this', 'yeh but I think this 'no but I think this' blah blah blah, with little 'that's an interesting point, tell me more about it'.

The trick is this...

If someone pushes you in communication don't Push back (our conditioned response), Pull; ask some questions, try and gain rapport, and when you understand their world well enough, then go to Push. They are more likely to go with you because you've taken the time to understand them. In the words of the Management Guru Steve Covey 'seek first to understand before being understood'.

That's it... said it was simple! The hard bit is changing your embedded behaviour. Most people I know (not all) naturally Push back when pushed and have to practice asking a question or two before they Push. The more you practice the more the new behaviour will become conditioned. In fact, when you notice you are messing up and think 'god dammit I should have asked more questions' then you are learning Push and Pull. If you don't notice you are messing up, you probably are messing up unconsciously!

If you change the balance to favour more Pull than Push (try at least 60% Pull) your influencing skills will dramatically improve.

I'll give some examples of Push Pull in action later so you can try and squeeze them into the context of your life.

Examples Push Pull behaviours

Pull behaviours

- Good personal energy, in the right state of mind
- Ask questions and listen well
- Take time to build relationships
- Gain rapport, find common ground as per Dr Birdwhistell
- Seek first to understand before being understood
- Intrigued by people's behaviour rather than threatened

Push behaviours

- Persuade with key benefits. Using too many benefits can dilute the key points
- Occasionally disguise Push in a Pull by putting a solution in a question i.e. 'What would happen if you did XYZ' - I'll explain in Push tips soon (Hidden Push)
- Assert in a calm non-aggressive way

Tips on Push Pull

The tips on Pull far outweigh the tips on Push as I believe this is where you should spend the majority of your time.

Pull – tips/examples

Build relationships

Practice your rapport skills, try out new ways of presenting with Visual/Auditory/Kinaesthetic elements. Practice reading body language. Pick someone in your workplace who you think could have a positive effect on your career, then try and build a relationship.

Become intrigued by people's behaviour. Quite often others can frustrate and annoy us which causes a negative reaction in our mind, which in turn cancels out any potential of rapport, thus leading to a lack of influence. Being intrigued by someone is a positive emotion which can lead to discovery and could help rapport. Surely you've had an experience where you started off really disliking someone then realised after a while you liked them. People are usually not what they initially seem, you need to dig deeper to gain understanding... Pull

Practice your questioning technique

When you ask questions practice asking open questions. How do you ask an open question? That was an open question! Open questions gently make the other person give you more information. Closed questions can lead to a yes or no answer.

Example of a closed question:

'Did that cause you an issue'? - answer 'yes or no' - a closed question.

Same situation with an open question:
'What issues did that cause you'? answer unlikely to be yes or no as that would be odd. They are likely to tell you the issues.

How, Who, Why, What, When open questions up... adding 'tell me more' can make it warmer.

'Tell me, what issue did that cause you'?

Be careful of Why as it can sound like an accusation, especially if you emphasise the Why in the sentence. Don't get me wrong asking Why we do things is a great question, however, be aware of the culture you are in as some people might feel interrogated.

I'm not trying to sell one of my other books but asking questions gets you beneath people's icebergs (a metaphor for how behaviour works). What you are seeing is just the tip of the iceberg, you need to dig deeper to find the real essence of what's driving the iceberg. All this and more in my '**A Guide to Motivation, Happiness, Success and Resilience**'.

Use perceptual positions before a meeting of importance

Perceptual positions is an easy powerful way of Pulling before you go into any meeting of importance where you need to be on your influencing 'A' game. It gives you a potential 360-degree insight prior to meetings to help shape your strategy.

To use perceptual positions, you ask questions (Pull) from 3 perspectives prior to a meeting.

Position 1 You

It's extremely useful to get clear on what you want prior to a meeting. This can be particularly important to those type of people who put others first all the time (people pleasers).

Examples:

- What do you want/need?
- What would be a good result from this meeting?
- What would make me happy?
- What's my bottom line?
- What are my killer persuasion points?
- What will I assert on?

Position 2:

This is where you sit in someone else's shoes, get into their world of thinking. By thinking like someone you immediately build empathy and rapport (even before you've met them). We are creatures of habit who spend most of our day thinking the same way. Thinking like someone else shakes us out of unconscious autopilot and gives us new insights.

Examples

- What do they want/need?
- What would they think a good result from this meeting would be?
- What would make them happy?
- What's their bottom line?
- What will be their areas of persuasion?
- What will they assert on?

Position 3

Now you have seen both sides, you get some independent advice. You can either describe position 1 & 2 to a colleague or friend and listen to their advice; or if you have no one around you put both positions up on the wall, step back, review and give yourself advice.

Examples

- Based on both sides what advice would you give me?
- Based on both sides what advice would I give myself (if you are alone)?
- What's this telling me?
- What insights can I derive from this?
- What would be a win/win scenario?
- What's my best strategy?

Energise yourself

Have you ever had a fabulous day in your life? I bet on those days you could influence anyone. I bet you were a Jedi knight!

Have you ever had a crappy day in your life? I bet your Jedi Influencing skills let you down on that day.

When you feel energised your whole message comes across in an impactful way. When you feel like shit, people can see it in your body and tone of language. In my view, how you feel when you are trying to influence is the most crucial factor. If you don't think I'm right think about the last time you felt rubbish and list all the things you gained influence on; I'm pretty sure it will be a short list.

Quick tips on getting energised (best to do this in the loo as people may judge you):

- Put your arms up in the air like you've won a race
- Bounce up and down with a massive smile
- Sit in the cubicle and picture the outcome you want from the meeting (like you are watching the scene unfold in a cinema. You are in the seat watching you on the screen)
- Read my book '**A Guide to Motivation, Success, Happiness & Resilience**' Details of the above and many other, dare I say, 'cool' ideas are in there

Push – tips/examples

Tentative ideas

'I'm not sure what you think, but what about doing it this way'?

Suggested proposals

'Can I suggest we do this'?

Persuasion

'Can I suggest we do this as the benefits will be XYZ'. Try and stick to your killer sales benefits, if you add too many people may lose your key persuasion points.

Assertion

If you get the balance of Push Pull right you should rarely need to go into assertion. When you do go into assertion be aware you only have one bullet so use it wisely.

For example, a Manager dealing with a member of staff

'If you do that again I will put you on a disciplinary warning'.

The reply could be

A) 'Fair enough boss, I won't do it again'– the assert has worked

B) 'I think you are wrong and I don't care what you think'- the assert hasn't worked, so the Manager must follow through or lose all credibility

Before you got to this position a good deal of Pulling may have avoided the situation completely.

For example:

'Tell me about your involvement in this incident'?
'What impact has your behaviour had on everyone'?
'What do you propose we do about this situation'?

Once you have heard their full view on the situation you could if necessary move to assert, at least you know you will be on solid ground.

When and if you do go to assert, you need to be calm, clear, short and to the point with upright, open, confident body language. In the chapter on body language I talked about it being weird to stare at people all the time, this is a small exception. As this is a short statement it should go with good strong eye contact.

For example

'We will do it X way, otherwise Z will happen'.

'I've listened to, and heard everything you have to say, and this is what I'm saying is going to happen, otherwise the consequences will be XYZ'.

If you do move to assertion try not to weaken it by being gushy immediately after the assertive statement as it loses the assertive edge.

For example

'We will do X, otherwise the implication will be Z ....
is that alright; I hope its not too difficult, how's the
family'?

Bonus tip on push

This is a useful way of planting a suggestion in
someone's head without them initially pushing it
away, and/or putting an idea across that you are not
confident with.

You - Push by asking it as a 'what would happen if'?
question.

So, if you wanted to push the idea of everyone having
as much holiday as they want at work which would
probably be ridiculed and pushed back. You could say
'what would happen if everyone were allowed to have
as much holiday as they wanted'? This way people
would have to think about the question, which means
you won't get an immediate push back, they will give
you their response. Their response may still be a no
but they are more likely to consider the question
properly, which could start a healthy debate. They
may say 'actually I've heard that peak performers
thrive with autonomy and as long as we employ
people with the right attitude, we will be awesome'.

Examples of Push Pull in action

The supermarket nightmare

Have you ever seen a child and parent kicking off in a supermarket? This is a classic example of how not to use Push, which can lead to a lifetime of hell for the parent and, in the end, the child.

Child – 'Can I have some sweets please; I've been a good boy today' (persuasive Push)

Parent – 'No you can't because it's your dinner when we get home and it will ruin your appetite' (firm persuasive Push).

Child – 'Pleeeeeasssse can I have some sweets; I promise to eat all my dinner' (desperate persuasive Push).

Parent – 'No you can't you said that last time and didn't eat your dinner, stop causing a fuss or there will be trouble' (assertive Push).

Child – 'I want some sweets' (assertive Push).

Parent – 'No' (shouty parent).

Child screams and wails on the floor (bat shit crazy Push).

Parent – 'If you carry on no more sweets ever again' (highly assertive, or the nuclear Push; no Christmas presents, more likely to be demonstrated in supermarkets around the world in December).

Child – 'I hate you' (out of control Push).

Parent – 'If you calm down and promise to eat your dinner you can have a small sweet' (panicked persuasive Push).

Child begins to calm down and gets some sweets.

I've got 3 kids and would always be cautious of giving advice to parents about parenting as it can be such a challenge. With the first kid you've got no idea what to do, the second you are far calmer and relaxed, the third, far too lazy.

If you've got kids you probably remember having your first child and getting advice from your non child friends on how to bring up kids, only to see them fall on their arse once they had their first one. I remember this one from some of my non parent friends; as my kids were watching TV or playing war games...'When I have children they're not going to watch TV or play with toy guns'. Visualise that in the most patronising voice possible and try to avoid punching them on the nose.

So, if you are a parent, take or leave this advice, I appreciate I don't know your world!

In the previous scenario a Push was immediately met with a Push, which escalated very quickly, and then led to an ultimate Push of no sweets ever or no Christmas presents. A Push most parents would never follow through with. So, the child learns that as long as they Push hard enough the parent may threaten but, in the end, will give way. They then carry this through into the rest of their life and into work. When they get to work, they still behave as a Push child, which eventually pisses people off and becomes a career threat. If you watch programmes like Super Nanny, they suggest you get clear on your boundaries and stick to them. If you do go to a strong Push, you have to stick to it. So, get clear on your boundaries/rules and delete the rules that can't be followed through such as no sweets or Christmas presents.

I once heard an interview with a Dad of sextuplets being asked what advice he would give to parents. His reply: 'Have as few rules as possible and stick to them'.

In the Supermarket scenario perhaps a bit of coaching/relationship building and questioning before entering the supermarket.

Parent - 'Before we go to the supermarket what rules shall we agree'? Once agreed stick to them no matter what.

Or, if in the supermarket the child says, 'can I have some sweets please I've been a good boy'?

Parent Pulls – 'You have been a good boy, what happened the last time you had sweets before your tea'?

Child replies 'I didn't eat my tea, but I promise to eat it this time'.

The Parent has some choices:

1. The child is not having sweets

If your choice is this kid is definitely not having sweets, then say so calmly and stick to it whatever pandemonium occurs. Whilst you will be as embarrassed as hell your child will learn the boundaries and the next time should be better or, if not, the next time after that as the child becomes conditioned. If you give in, your short-term release from the stress and embarrassment could be replaced by a lifetime of behavioural hell.

2. The child will end up having sweets

If you were always going to give the child sweets, then make the child work for it by using Pull.

'How many sugar calories should we decide on'? ... that could make it a little educational!

'What shall we agree if you have sweets and don't eat your tea'?

'How would you feel about choosing some sweets and having them after dinner'?

Please don't get me wrong, I wouldn't dream of telling you how to bring up your kids or suggest this is a fool-proof approach. I can however pretty much guarantee that it will be more effective than the nuclear option of 'no sweets ever' or 'no Christmas presents' unless you are as hard as nails!

Mum/Dad, can I have some help with my homework?

One more on the kids! If you have kids no doubt you have come across this scenario.

8pm at night.

Child - 'Mum/Dad, can I have some help with my homework'? Or 'can I have some help to build my school project volcano'? Or 'can I have some help with my school poem recital'? etc. (Pull)

Parent - 'sure when does it need to be done by'? (Pull).

Child - 'tomorrow...'. (nervous Push).

Parent - 'WTF'. usually in their head (not cool to swear at your kids) 'Why are you asking at this late hour, how long have you known about this'? (use of accusational 'Why' Pull).

Child - 'I forgot' (mouse like Push - I'm in the shit).

Parent - 'I am sick and tired of you doing this, I work hard all day, I give you everything you want and all I ask is a little respect, I'm tired of being treated like a dogsbody'. blah blah blah'.

This then either goes two ways:

1) The child withdraws and stops asking the parent for things in the future when they know they have messed up. If you are a parent would you really want your child to stop talking to you when they get in trouble?

2) The child Pushes back, and a night of pandemonium occurs.

Either option is not good. A bit of Pull may save the day.

A real-life example from my life:

9.30pm after a long day travelling and working in London:

My youngest - 'Dad can you help me with my lines for the school play' (Pull)

Me - 'Sure thing when does it need to be done by'? (Pull)

My youngest - 'Tomorrow' (tentative Push)

Me - 'WTF (in my head), you're kidding me, I can't believe you're asking 9.30 at night the day before, how long have you known about this, why are you asking now'? (Raised voice accusational Push).

My youngest - 'Sorry, don't worry I'll do it by myself' (Not sure if sulky or apologetic Push).

Me - 'No, it's OK let's crack on and get it done' (dutiful parent Push).

We proceed to attempt to learn the lines, however he seems to be struggling and I find myself getting grumpy when he gets the lines wrong 'If you had given us more notice we wouldn't be having to rush this would we'? (Dick head Push).

Then I have a moment of insight (I had been running a communication course that day), I can feel myself getting seriously grumpy, I'm tired, I've had a long day, but it dawns on me if this continues both of us are going to be unhappy, I'll feel guilty for being grumpy, and he won't learn his lines and probably won't ask for help again.

Me - 'Let's stop for a second and reset. How can we do this and have some fun' (energising Pull).

My youngest - 'I'm not sure' (slight mind set change - intrigued Push).

Me - 'What would happen if you walk around the room reciting your lines and every time you get it wrong I throw a paper ball at you'? (Pull but really a disguised Push – I had been getting people in the course during the day to throw paper balls)

My youngest - 'sounds fun'

And off we went, he walked around reciting and I threw paper balls which made him laugh in hysterics until he had learnt his lines.

Did he announce homework at the last minute again? Yes, he's a kid!

If your Boss comes at you in an angry state

Your boss - 'I can't believe you've allowed us to get into this situation, it makes me doubt your competence' (angry boss Push).

Pull reply (ask a question). 'Ok, I can see you are very upset, can you tell me a bit more about what has gone wrong'?

If you Push back you have a higher chance of inflaming the situation. If you Pull, you get to understand the facts the boss is using (in their world). If the facts are correct and you've messed up, I suggest you apologise and fix it. If the facts are wrong, you can give the boss the correct facts and start a discussion.

You are one of those people who doesn't like to say no:

Your boss keeps piling extra work on you and you struggle to say no.

Example: Your boss says, 'can we get this done please'? (quite often your boss will ask for things without considering the priority of all the other things on the go at the moment.... maybe their boss has asked them for something, and they are just passing it on).
Usual response will be 'when would you like it by'? which is a question and is Pull and is better than just saying 'sure thing'. It however does imply that you will do it.
A better Pull might be 'OK, how does it fit in with the priority of XYZ'; this way the boss can see the workload and decide what comes first. If you have an unreasonable boss who expects everything to be done and is working you to death you could ask more direct questions such as, 'I only have capacity for XYZ which one do you want me to drop'? If they continue to be unreasonable perhaps look for another job. If you are just lazy, then your boss is probably being reasonable!

A peer or someone at work asking for unreasonable requests

A typical example could be a salesperson asking a marketing team to put a campaign together for a client.

Salesperson –'The client would like XYZ by next week for the discounted price of £x, I appreciate it's quite short notice but this is an important client and could lead to a massive deal, if we can't do it they will go elsewhere'.

This is against the internal agreed process and price controls (sorry salespeople a common scenario!!).

You as the marketing person may quite rightly say 'there is no way we can turn it around in those timescales and its completely out of line with our pricing and agreed process. We will lose money on this deal'. You've probably heard the salesperson use this line many times in the past.

The salesperson then gets grumpy, throws their toys out of their pram, goes to their boss who goes to your boss and whilst you are right to say no, a pile of shit has occurred and with that pile of shit usually comes pooey fallout.

You could try:

'How does this fit in with our agreed process and pricing'? This gets the salesperson to wake up from autopilot which may change future behaviour, or you could get more info from the salesperson which may lead to an alternative way of dealing with the situation;
'what's the client trying to achieve, what's their end game'? Once you have the full information you could keep on Pulling. 'We only have so many hours in a day, which one of your other clients do you want us to deprioritise'?

Buying a car

Get some rapport with the salesperson. People are more likely to give you a deal if they like you. The salesperson is more than likely to try and get rapport with you, but that's just them working you... give it back to them, they will have no idea that you are doing it.

When they start discussing the price, they may get you to give them a ballpark figure of your budget by asking questions (they are Pulling).

Just side-track the questions and ask a question back.

'What's your best price'?

They may ramble for a bit and come back with a price. Observe their body language, they will give clues that that's not necessarily the best price.

Stay in Pull 'I understand everything you've said and how cool this deal is but... what's your best price'?

Keep going until they look congruent when they say their best price.

Selling

If you are a professional salesperson Push Pull should fit into any sales technique you've learned whether that be AIDA, DIPIDA, SPIN or any other acronym used to describe a sales questioning technique.

I have spent many years observing hundreds of sales calls. I have seen the good, the bad and the ugly (one day I knew I would find a way of referencing this Spaghetti western film).

The most common salesperson development need I have observed is this:

Salespeople by nature have been recruited because they have natural ability to get on with people and build rapport, which is a key part of Pull. However, you often see this scenario in observed sales calls:

1. A salesperson builds rapport beautifully - Pull

2. A salesperson then presents what they have to offer – persuasive Push.

If the client by luck needs exactly what the salesperson has to offer, then the sale proceeds.

More often than not the client wants time to think, probably because the product for sale doesn't quite match the deep-down needs/wants of the client. Because the salesperson hasn't asked enough questions (Pull) they haven't found out what the client's deeper needs/wants are and therefore can't match the product to them. So, if you are a salesperson and you find that quite a lot of calls don't lead to sales then maybe consider adding to your sales technique portfolio by asking more questions. Once you have a deeper understanding of the client's needs/wants you can match your product to them.

If you just did one thing!

There is no way I could guess what examples you would want me to write about to cover your needs/wants. If we were sitting together and you were describing a situation you were struggling to influence; I would probably ask you to describe the situation in full (Pull). When you'd described the situation, I'd be more than likely to say 'were you Pulling or Pushing in that scenario. 8 times out of 10 you would say I was Pushing. I'd then say 'how could you to turn that Push into a Pull'? (that's a Pull). If you were unsure, I'd say 'what would happen if you said this'? (hidden Push). On reflection most people find they are Pushing, a simple switch to Pull makes the world of difference.

If you practice asking one or two more questions every time someone Pushes.... you will become a Jedi knight of influence in no time

One final tip to embed Push Pull into your behaviour.

Every time you go to a meeting, on your notepad (physical or digital) write the word Pull at the top. This will remind you to ask questions and gain rapport. If you do this for a few weeks, it will become an embedded habit.

In conclusion:

- Words have little meaning; it's how you say it and what you say with your body
- People like people who are like them; to gain rapport be like them
- The majority of people have a stronger preference for Visual & Kinaesthetic; show and do as well as tell
- When giving presentations build in MMIs (kinaesthetic)
- Be aware of the impact you have with your body language as well as reading others'
- Before you try and influence get in the right state not a right state
- Pull before you Push

I don't pretend to be a writer; these books are merely a guide based on my experience of working with 10,000+ people around the world. Please feel free to rate and give feedback on this book. All reviews are gratefully received... they give me a motivational kick for the next one!

All the best and thanks for reading.

Gavin

Notes

Notes

Notes

Printed in Great Britain
by Amazon